Dr. MARCUS D. BLAKEMORE

Knoxville, Tennessee

Vol. 1

To: Tedd
My good friend
Thanks for all that
you do.
4/16/2018

October 31, 2008 - May 25 2009, 4:22 p.m.

Dr. MARCUS D. BLAKEMORE

Minster Marcus D. Blakemore

Where to Turn

When You Don't Know Where to Turn

In Modern Times

Vol. 1

For more information or suggestions, please contact:

Dry Ink Media & Publishing

marcusblakemore@hotmail.com

www.marcusblakemore.com

BIOGRAPHICAL SKETCH

I, Marcus D. Blakemore, am a native of Chattanooga, Tennessee. My wife, Heather Sumpter Blakemore hails from Altadena, California. We have two wonderful daughters Jade and Clarke. I have a half brother named Aaron Sanders, niece Teonna Sanders and a half sister Petra "Peaches" Mitchel.

I was raised in a Christian home by my mother Beverly A. Blakemore, my aunt Carolyn D. Green and my grandparents John and Lula Mae Nash, I accepted the Lord in my life at the age of 13. My grandmother Lula was the cornerstone of faith in our home. Additionally, my mother instilled the values of divine patience. My aunt carried the strength of Paul; and my grandfather had the wisdom of Solomon. The spiritual lifestyles they lead gave me the inspiration to proceed on a path of transforming life's challenges Gods way.

Currently, I am an associate pastor at Mount Calvary Baptist Church in Knoxville, Tennessee. I serve in several areas at my church under the leadership of Pastor Leroy Franklin. The areas of service that God has placed me in include leading the Men's fellowship group, teaching a Sunday school class, and assisting with the Vacation Bible school committees.

The works of the Lord are great,
Studied by all who have pleasure in them.
His work is honorable and glorious,
And His righteousness endures forever.
Psalm 111:2-4

DEDICATION

To God, thank you for having an unchanging heart. I am grateful to you for sending Jesus to our rescue. I can feel the warmth of your joy when I restored myself and my family to you. To my loving wife Heather, thank you for your creative ideas and your management of our home while I was attending school full time. I enjoy the things we do together. God has given us nine years, and it is incredible that those many years have passed so quickly! Through the changing phases of our lives, "we are still together ☺!" To Jade and Clarke, I will continue to teach you about your heavenly Father -- almighty God, so that when I am not around, you will both trust Him to continue to lead you. Aunt Carolyn and Uncle Nay, thank you for showing me the commitments of marriage. To my cousin Corlan Green, you are the greatest, and I am excited that you love God. To my nieces and nephew, Teonna Sanders, Madison, and Xavier Sumpter everything you do remember, do it God's way and He will reward you. The Washington's: Uncle George, Aunt Girdie, Audrey, Seth, Kelly and Kirby King, thanks for accepting me in the family. All of you all have shown me the power of education in the secular and spiritual environment. To my father-in-law George Sumpter, I could not ask for a better father-in-law. You have been a true father figure to me. I am appreciative of your openness, and I value our relationship. To my brother-in-law Greg, you have taught me to stay on course for God -- I love you. Grandma Sumpter, I admire your diligence and your vigor. At age 86, you are an inspiration to us all. You have demonstrated that citizen involvement in its many forms is an effective way to express concern and support, having just returned from an education rally at the March on Washington May 16, 2009. Thank you for all your phone calls and encouragement. Aunt Ethel, thank you for always having Beaufort open for vacation. Kevin and Mary Downes thanks for the comfort during the holidays, especially Christmas dinner. To my church family, men's fellowship group and Sunday school class at Mount Calvary Baptist Church under Pastor Leroy Franklin's leadership, thanks for all the many prayers and blessings you have expressed on me and my family's behalf. The emphasis of education has paid off for me. Thanks to Dr. J. Harvey Gillespie, Tammi Gwinn-Campbell, and Cameron Molchan for advising me through this process. Many thanks to Masonic Lodge Geometry 410 and the greatest fraternity in the world Iota Alpha Chapter, Omega Psi Phi Inc. To my friends listed below who believed and supported me in all my endeavors Mr. and Mrs. Marwin Smith, Rev. Joseph Smith, Rev. James Billings and his mother Geraldine Billings (for those thirty course lunch meals), Rev. Eric Bonner and Central Church of Christ, Mr. and Mrs.

Sam Anderson, Aaron Anderson, Joan Murray, Myron Austin, (the ladies of influence, Antwaun Jackson, Crystal Howard, Nikki and Myron Hendley, Sulema Lewis, LaKendra Moore); (M-5 Larry Williams, Shango Cooke, Darrow Davenport, Carlie Young); (Junto Bros – Ralph Tate, Justin Rosser); (Tax Professionals - Jim Lee and Doe Crocker); (Shanklin and Sons); (ETMC- Mark Deathridge); (B&B Baffin Harper); Reginald Sutton, (Mike and Tammy's Fried Green Tomatoes, Scotts Place and Magnolia Café-Tony Kimbrough for the days my family was too tired to cook while working on this paper); Margie Loyd, Laharvi Gwin, Tony Sapp, Derrick Thomas, Francis Harper, Revonda Moody, Coop, John Wright, Hallern Hilton Hill , LaVoice Reese, Raleigh Wynn, John Jordan, Joseph Askew, Darnel "Boo" Adams, Rick and April Hardin, Albert Harris, Mr. and Mrs. Andre James, Mr. and Mrs. Tommy Wykle, Mr. and Mrs. David Martin, Mr. and Mrs. John Frazier, Stacy Eubanks, (Radio show, Business on Demand, Robert Mintor and Tatia Harris) TNT Digital Printing- Tony Turman, Rufus Rodgers, Mr. and Mrs. Todd Kelly, Albert Baah, Randol Turman, Dr. Thomas Haskins, Charles and Beverly Holland (thanks for allowing your daughter to babysit our children), Jay Vincent, Men's Proverbs Group, Mr. and Mrs. Mark Brown, Zakiyah Modeste, Saidah and Denecko Kinerman, Kelli White, Mr.and Mrs. Stan Johnson, Over Tha Topp Motorcycle Club and Gene Parks. Most of all to my mother, Beverly Blakemore I cannot thank you enough for showing me Jesus in your life. Aunt Carolyn and I joked about your weakness when it came to people. However it was nothing but God in your life and Jesus as your role model, showing us His strength. Momma I am filled with deep gratitude. I can truly see what God has done not only for you, but also for me.

Table of Contents

INTRODUCTION

When your patterns of life have come to a dead end where do you go? What is your thought process? How do you make a wise decision? Better yet, how do you stay focused while being over whelmed? It is easy to live life when the course is going good. We live a lifestyle listening and adopting secular and spiritual concepts and all too often, the same secular and spiritual conceptual adoptions fail you and me. Where do we go from there? How do we handle exposure, experiences and astonishments? Rick Warren, author of *"The Purpose Driven Life"*, asked the same question in his book. He questions, "What do you do when God seem a million miles away? It is easy to worship God when things are going great in your life – when He has provided food, family, health, and happy situations. But circumstances are not always pleasant. How do you worship God then?"[i]

What about someone who has had a secular person as their mentor, and now that person they looked up to has been showing them a dead end? Robert Chew asked the question in a Time magazine article, "But what can you do?[ii] Robert Chew and his family lost a combined total of nearly 30 million dollars investing with Bernie L Madoff, of Bernie L. Madoff Investment Securities. They had been investing for over two decades. Bernie L. Madoff was a well known financial advisor to thousands of people who placed their fortune and faith in him. Mr. Madoff created an illusion of financial investment for over forty years and had taken up to fifty billion dollars from people to invest with his firm. Robert Chew identified motives within himself that always lure a person when their attentions are on the wrong things. Robert said "with a combination of pleasure and trepidation" [iii], he handed over his family's life savings to invest with Madoff. A proverb states that "He who will trust in his riches will fall, but the righteous will flourish like foliage"[iv]. The majority of the investors were not wealthy people; but were hard working, blue collar people, who saved their money. When the time came they took their life savings to invest with Bernie Madoff for added security. When the tide came after twenty plus years, people found out they had been robbed, they had not only put their trust in Madoff but their faith as well.

Even the spiritual side has its victims. The Honorable Elijah Muhammad, the past leader of the Nation of Islam, had twenty two children and a majority of the children were outside of marriage. However, the teachings from the Quran says "...And those who guard their private parts, except from their wives or those their right hands possess, - for indeed, they are not to be blamed – But whoever seeks beyond that, then they are the transgressors." [Quran: 70:29-31]. Malcolm X was a follower of the Honorable Elijah Muhammad.   There were two women who served as secretaries to the Honorable Elijah Muhammad. These women were petitioning in the cold with their children to the Honorable Elijah Muhammad for him to take care of them. Malcolm X witnessed what was unfolding from his spiritual mentor, the Honorable Elijah Muhammad. Imam Wallace Warith and Malcom X consulted the Honorable Elijah Muhammad about his actions. The Honorable Elijah Muhammad replied to his son, Imam Wallace Warith and Malcolm in an article stating "his wife, Clara, was dead to him, like Khadijah, the wife of the original Prophet Muhammad, and likewise Elijah felt divinely sanctioned to seek out virgins to produce good seed."[v] So, where does a spiritual individual turn when they have a broken heart from their mentor like the Honorable Elijah Muhammad? "Elijah Muhammad's response left Malcolm X dissatisfied and contributed to his growing disenchantment with the nation of Islam"[vi].

Past and present modern times have brought comfort to things that were viewed immoral in the past it seems. These concepts are not born with an individual, but are attached and molded to an individual according to his or her environmental concept and lifestyle.

I am confident about life, however it is difficult staying on course when life slaps you in the face, gut punches and kicks you in the rear. While in seminary, reality is that I have been one hundred percent focused on my studies. Since the Devil knows this, he has tried to throw everything in my way to discourage and distract me. When Paul says we must die daily, I fully understand. While in my second week of this assignment my mother's home was burglarized. I was to appear in traffic court the next day, and not only that, Thanksgiving was only a day away. So, you can visualize the kind of dilemma I faced. During the third week in my home, the main sewer drain line was blocked and all the toilets, sinks, and bath tubs were backed up. My final exams were the very next day, I had two papers due, and in addition, I faced two flat tires that Monday morning when I walked out to take my daughter to school. I was really overwhelmed, facing my own doctoral thesis: "Where To Turn, When You Don't Know Where To Turn In Modern Times." I had to let go and stay focused on my assigned task from my Father, and it was not easy! It all seemed an over burden, however my mother was unharmed, the judge remembered me from a political fundraiser, it turned out to be one of the best Thanksgivings I had ever had, we were able to get the drains unblocked, I had time to study for my exams, get my papers completed, and my wife and children were still alive and healthy. The reality was that my situation needed only a little adjustment for a positive outcome to result.

On the path of life, in modern times, everyone will encounter trials, storms, setbacks, and simple challenges to their ethical standards. Today's modern life and times are poles apart from the past life experienced by our friends, parents, and mentors. With the help of modern innovations, times are even vastly different from three years to six months ago. It seems our world, and its environment changes at the speed of light, but life situations remain the same. While there appears to be a constant need for direction, very rarely do we seek to find the main source of the answer. In the years of 2007 through 2009, the United States of America was involved in the largest financial disasters ever. Citizens thought that power and prosperity was the back bone of our country. Yet, with each passing year, God had been taken from the foundation. Prayer had been taken out of school, the Ten Commandments were taken out of the court rooms, public, and federal buildings. When terrorist attacked United States of America on September 11, 2001, God became an anchor once more. God was quickly accepted back in the classrooms, government buildings, and many other places of business. However, as the terrorist alert seemed to fade, many people in our country have become comfortable once more, God was released from America once more and the time for strong leadership was needed to turn the country around. Only a few were saying God was missing from the foundation. The media, citizens, and community leaders wanted a new President. Where does the nation of the United States turn now? Just like Israel in similar situations a military threat, corruption and the God put of commission. The people of the United States of America wanted a new King. President Barack Obama was chosen and he did acknowledge God and had prayer before breakfast at his inauguration. After that God was only heard about when the President concluded at the end of a speech or interview.

In I Samuel Chapter 8, Israel also wanted a new King. After suffering defeat at the hands of the Philistines, the Israelites brought out the Ark of the Covenant and took it into battle with them, convinced this will bring victory. As we see, it did not. Now in chapter 8, we saw it was not the Ark, but a king in whom the Israelites would place their faith and trust. They ignored God's word from Samuel and wanted to turn in their own way. Their reason just as now in the United States they wanted a new king.

The modern times we live in now give concepts of self-help, do-it yourself, or self-independence. The basis for self-help is often self-reliance from any individual, environmental realm or spirituality. The outcome births from a substantial modern world view concept or spiritual concept. Outcomes from the last four decades were closed minded. A certain culture could tell people where they could shop, dine or live in the same community. Now, those same realities are driven by overt missions. However, the overt concept goes both ways, secular and spiritual. The overt concept can be viewed in both spiritual and secular ways. This idea reflects the constancy of the human spirit from the past to modern times. The highway of the upright is to depart from evil: he that keepeth his way preserveth his soul. Proverbs 16:17 [vii]

The modern world view concepts, give the support for secular need, materialism, physical attraction, mental, emotional and a higher authority within self. The modern world view concepts, shows us the wide road ahead which can be seen, felt, and touched without strings attached. Things like fornication, little white lies, soft porn, fowl language, revenge and misconceptions. Everything in this view seems to have a solid foundation. The spiritual environmental concept supports the reverse of the secular concept. In the direction for needs, physically, mentally, emotionally, affection and comfort, the spiritual lifestyle is to be renewed in your mind, soul and spirit through an unseen higher calling. The spiritual environmental concept shows us the narrow road ahead which it seems it cannot be seen, felt, and touched. This concept seems to have strings attached, it seems to require daily reading of the Bible, daily prayer, church attendance, and believing in an unseen god. This concept takes relying on ourselves and materials out of the center of survival. The spiritual environmental concept view seems to have an unseen foundation. This view gives the foundation of hope instead of a material of substance that would withstand a storm in one's life. In the world concepts, if you are injured call the late Johnnie Cochran law firm. The spiritual concept says "But I tell you not to resist an evil person. But whoever slaps you on your cheek, turn the other to him as also".[viii]

Most of us have all read about the three little pigs, this story is about how a mother who sent her three little piglet sons into the world to seek their fortune. They each built their homes out of three different materials; brick, straw, and sticks. It turns out that only one pig's home was built with material strong enough to withstand the evil of the wolf. This story reflects my thought that our lives are the same way based on what we choose to build our foundations from and the direction we are going in this road of life.

The world view concept, leads individuals to worldly desires, disobedience, materialism, greed, violence, hypocrisy, lust, pride, envy, idolatry, hate, selfishness, cheating, gossip, lying, and unfortunately many more. The spiritual environmental concept guides individuals to love, joy, peace, patience, kindness, goodness, faithfulness, gentleness and self-control. The environmental concept you live in will either birth in the individual the spiritually or what the world has to offer. When an individual takes on reality, they will choose which seems to be good and acceptable and perfect in either the spirituality or worldly conceptual realm.

The end result is that when your spirituality or worldly concepts in modern times cannot give answers, when you don't know where to turn. We must embrace our concepts from a different paradigm. We must not allow current difficulties or current illusions in modern times to lower our expectations of what can be done, or deter us from doing what must be done. While sitting on the road idly asking yourself where to turn, this doctoral thesis will give biblical vs. secular; observational strategy, concepts, realities, Father figure, discipline, love, peace and rejuvenation in turning to the correct direction, where to turn, when you don't know, where to turn.

Chapter I

Functions of Your Own Understanding
Where to Turn

When I left home and enrolled at Knoxville College, I put in gear my own understanding for life as soon as my parents waved goodbye. In my mind, I thought I had figured out the formula for life and embraced my concepts. According to Webster's dictionary, a concept is something conceived in the mind: Thought, notion, it also states a concept is an abstract or generic idea generalized from particular instances. My concept definition was, to do whatever it took to become successful in life. To trust no one and always go over and beyond to make things happen. I was so excited that there was no one that could tell me how to live. I would show my parents that my way of life would lead to success. When I made a decision it would be all about how I made it on my own. I had a great childhood. With that great childhood, I also had all the ups and downs in my childhood while growing up. My grandmother use to say a Proverb to me all the time when I tried to figure something out. "Trust in the Lord with all your heart, and lean not on your own understanding; in all your ways acknowledge Him, and He shall direct your paths." Proverbs 3:5-6. That first night in college as I lay in my bed, I saw the concepts I had picked up. I thought my conceptual understanding would bring freedom, prosperity, peace and avenues from a broken heart of past disappointments. All the concepts that made me feel good I kept. All the concepts that made me feel bad or uncomfortable I would alter and learn from as lessons learned in my past life. All the concepts that I was unsure of I tucked in the dark corners of my heart. When I woke up that morning life was never the same again. My life understanding of my own concepts began on the multi- cultural campus of Knoxville College and the road was wide.

My spiritual concepts were the first to be challenged. They were the first to be lived less. I, Marcus Blakemore, the proper talking, southern hospitality, clean dressed, educated fellow from Chattanooga, Tennessee, fell off the path fast. The environment was so saturated from other urban cultures; I was like a kid in the candy store. My behavior started forming in the environment that was tasteful to me at the time. The school campus was like all others I had visited. You had the smart students, spiritual students, popular students, adventurous students, and the naturalistic students. I choose to hang out with the popular and adventurous students. When I tried to bring my spiritual ethics there was no room for them. My spiritual belief was not embraced at all. My so-called friends at the time were not trying to hear those Ten Commandments. To them, it seemed like restraints. Day-by-day, I was becoming what I allowed myself to be in. I lowered my standards and accepted another concept. I unplugged my "GPS" God's Planned Strategy.

God's Planned Strategy "GPS"

God plans a strategy always in everyday life. The plan of strategy from God is given to us all; however some of us just do not follow His path. Priscilla Sapp explained this idea in her article "The Pillar of Prayer in Eastern Africa" Sapp said, a team was ministering in Southern Sudan, which has an expanded prayer network, and they were always alert to potential prayer partners. One of the team members was on a training safari through Tanzania. While staying in a home of a Tanzanian, they had the opportunity to share about their future work and plans in Southern Sudan. God moved the

Tanzanians to commit themselves to pray for these IMB (International Mission Board) workers of a different race, denomination, and cultural background. People worldwide are a part of this team's prayer network. Sapp goes on to say that Southern Sudan is not the safest place in the world to be. As the team leader began this ministry, there were moments of doubt that personnel would ever be added although there was great need. So a team member asked his prayer partners to begin praying for God to call out laborers, knowing it was God's field and His harvest. As a result, in only 18 months this team has added 15 members. God has called out 15 Godly men and women to choose to serve Him in a war zone. Although this team was well laid out with strategies and plans, an important part of choosing to make prayer a pillar in their strategy is laying those plans at the feet of Jesus and yielding to His leadership. As they were beginning a specific story strategy, they spent time in prayer and asked others to intercede. God intervened through an injury, a trip to the hospital, picking up a stranger and the conversation with him to change the course of their initial strategy. But through God's specific and perfect intervention, a better strategy and plan resulted, and God is using a story in a significant way to lead people to Himself, to disciple and to train them. God has a planned strategy we must yield to his leadership. The mission team had a planned strategy but God had the matter planned strategy called GPS.[ix]

Definition of GPS

Most people hear the Words GPS and think of Global Positioning System (GPS), which is a satellite-based navigation system made up of a network of 24 satellites placed into orbit by the U.S. Department of Defense. The GPS was originally intended for military applications, but in the 1980s, the government made the system available for civilian use.[x] The GPS works in any weather conditions, anywhere in the world, 24 hours a day. The GPS unit can be used in your car for turn-by-turn navigation with voice and visual guidance, as well as navigating off-road or on the water, with a variety of detailed mapping options available. The purpose of the GPS unit is to provide directions for your safety and to your destination without getting lost. It is a tool to help save time and deliver us from unsafe environmental conditions. Does this sound familiar to anything in life? Are the functions of the GPS similar to the Bible, Koran, the United States Constitution, a Mother and Fathers advice, or your employee handbook? Are the references I just mentioned advising the same things as the GPS?

Description of GPS

Gods Planned Strategy (GPS) is the GPS we are identifying with. God has given us the coordinates in life. Since the creation of the world God has given us the direction. In the book of Genesis, we find that God made the world one day at a time. We can see every time He made something, He designed a strategy for the next move. In Genesis Chapter II, we see how God was moving. "Now the Lord God had planted a garden in the east, in Eden; and there he put the man he had formed. And the Lord God made all kinds of trees grow out of the ground—trees that were pleasing to the eye and good for food. In the middle of the garden were the tree of life and the tree of the knowledge of good and evil." In the beginning of creation God gave man the planned strategy and like most of us, man left the path of righteousness and followed some other voice. Have you ever been in a car and following the GPS unit and your passenger say "No don't go that way, go that way it seems better".

Then you and your passenger end up in the wrong place because your passenger's directions sounded familiar, confident, and comfortable and perhaps, provided better scenery. The scripture in the Bible shows and the writer illustrates that this is what happened to Adam and Eve in the Garden of Eden. "The Lord God took the man and put him in the Garden of Eden to work it and take care of it. And the Lord God commanded the man, "You are free to eat from any tree in the garden; but you must not eat from the tree of the knowledge of good and evil, for when you eat of it you will surely die. The Lord God said, It is not good for the man to be alone. I will make a helper suitable for him. Now the Lord God had formed out of the ground all the beasts of the field and all the birds of the air. He brought them to the man to see what he would name them; and whatever the man called each living creature, that was its name. So the man gave names to all the livestock, the birds of the air and all the beasts of the field; but for Adam no suitable helper was found. So the Lord God caused the man to fall into a deep sleep; and while he was sleeping, he took one of the man's ribs and closed up the place with flesh. Then the Lord God made a woman from the rib he had taken out of the man, and he brought her to the man. The man said, "This is now bone of my bones and flesh of my flesh; she shall be called 'woman', for she was taken out of man". For this reason a man will leave his father and mother and be united to his wife, and they will become one flesh. The man and his wife were both naked, and they felt no shame."[xi] As we see, God made and directed the coordinates for the path of all living things. All we have to do his follow. Look at how the rivers, gardens, animals and people were all fine until they veered off the path. The snake was one animal that was just too smart for his own kind, which brings us to ourselves. Sometimes we are too smart for our own selves, read how Eve was enticed by the serpent.

"Now the serpent was craftier than any of the wild animals the Lord had made. He said to the woman, "Did God really say, 'You must not eat from any tree in the garden'?" The woman said to the serpent, "We may eat fruit from the trees in the garden, but God did say, 'You must not eat fruit from the tree that is in the middle of the garden, and you must not touch it, or you will die.' "You will not surely die," the serpent said to the woman "For God knows that when you eat of it your eyes will be opened, and you will be like God, knowing good and evil." When the woman saw that the fruit of the tree was good for food and pleasing to the eye, and also desirable for gaining wisdom, she took some and ate it. She also gave some to her husband, who was with her, and he ate it. Then the eyes of both of them were opened, and they realized they were naked; so they sewed fig leaves together and made coverings for themselves. Then the man and his wife heard the sound of the Lord God as he was walking in the garden in the cool of the day, and they hid from the Lord God among the trees of the garden. But the Lord God called to the man, "Where are you?" He answered, "I heard you in the garden, and I was afraid because I was naked; so I hid." And he said, "Who told you that you were naked? Have you eaten from the tree that I commanded you not to eat from?" The man said, "The woman you put here with me—she gave me some fruit from the tree, and I ate it." Then the Lord God said to the woman, "What is this you have done?" The woman said, "The serpent deceived me, and I ate." So the Lord God said to the serpent, "Because you have done this, "Cursed are you above all the livestock and all the wild animals! You will crawl on your belly and you will eat dust all the days of your life. And I will put enmity between you and the woman, and between your offspring and hers;

he will crush your head, and you will strike his heel." To the woman he said, "I will greatly increase your pains in childbearing; with pain you will give birth to children. Your desire will be for your husband, and he will rule over you. To Adam he said, "Because you listened to your wife and ate from the tree about which I commanded you, 'You must not eat of it,' "Cursed is the ground because of you; through painful toil you will eat of it all the days of your life. It will produce thorns and thistles for you and you will eat the plants of the field. By the sweat of your brow you will eat your food until you return to the ground, since from it you were taken; for dust you are and to dust you will return." Adam named his wife Eve, because she would become the mother of all the living. The Lord God made garments of skin for Adam and his wife and clothed them. And the Lord God said, "The man has now become like one of us, knowing good and evil. He must not be allowed to reach out his hand and take also from the tree of life and eat, and live forever." So the Lord God banished him from the Garden of Eden to work the ground from which he had been taken. After he drove the man out, he placed on the east side of the Garden of

Eden cherubim and a flaming sword flashing back and forth to guard the way to the tree of life."[xii]

Adam and Eve were given directions from the Source of Life. Like our passenger friend in the car giving directions, Adam and Eve listened to the wrong voice, just as when we listen to the wrong voice when we are out in the world, like listening to the passenger in the car about directions that are different from the global positioning system. God has left us direction. Are we adhering to them? There are some many things that can distract us from our path. I am sure when you are riding in your automobile you may make an unplanned stop because you saw the persuasive marketing sign, all you can eat, signup here it's free. That is the same thing that happened to Adam and Eve. Eve heard persuasive words and quickly followed, and so did Adam. God revealed the planned strategy and the plan was not followed.

We are all free to pursue God's plan or we can go our own way. God's plan is revealed not to harm you, but to give you hope and a future. In Jeremiah 29:11, when God made it clear to the Israelites, He says, "Then you will call upon me and come and pray to me, and I will listen to you. You will seek me and find me when you seek me with all your heart. I will be found by you, declares the Lord, and will bring you back from captivity." This is what the Lord says: "When seventy years are completed for Babylon, I will come to you and fulfill my gracious promise to bring you back to this place. For I know the plans I have for you," declares the Lord, "plans to prosper you and not harm you."

God has a planned strategy for us all, but it must be met with our faith in Him. When we put in our coordinates in a portable Garmin global positioning system, we are asking that we be taken to our destination safely. When we say our prayers to our God, our Father, we are asking to be taken to a destination safely. When the Garmin unit responds back to us with the directions, we examine and proceed to follow without hesitation. When our prayers have been answered and the directions have been given from God, the Bible, employee handbook, how well do we follow it?

Peter explains in Luke, Chapter V, that when he followed Jesus' plan for him to go fishing, it did not make any sense at the time. However, when Peter cast his net down as Jesus instructed, he brought it up so full that the net was breaking. It seems we are to just follow the scripture and God will provide. While we are wondering when is something going to happen, we must be certain that there is a divine plan for every life that is lived.

Daily most of us wonder what our purpose on this earth is. When I was in college, I did not have a clue at the time. I went about living in the world enjoying the fruits of the world and what it had to offer. God has a planned strategy for us but somehow we keep wondering off the path. Adam and Eve wondered off the path. They fell to the deception, as many of us today. The devil tried to deceive even Jesus, however Jesus quoted scripture to Himself and to the devil and He stayed on the path planned for Him. Solomon, the wisest man of all time, warns in Proverbs about staying on the path. The world has a planned strategy for us and it is compelled by the prince of darkness. The prince of darkness entices us to consent to the world. Solomon warns us about the evils of the world and what may entice us. God has left coordinates for us to follow. Will Gods Planed Strategy be followed by us like we follow Garmin? When you are lost where will you turn, when you don't know where to turn?

Cultural Concepts

The lifestyle we live comes from a cultural background we were born into, choose, or have been steered into. The lifestyle of the culture came from a conceived embraced concept. Webster dictionary defines a concept as something conceived in the mind; a thought, a notion. A concept is also an abstract or generic idea generalized from particular instances. Furthermore according to Webster dictionary the word conceived is to cause to begin: Originate (a project conceived by the company's founder), to take into one's mind. Concepts are also seen as Cultural views. The views or concepts are the drivers of our thinking, emotions, moral standards and beliefs. Some of these concepts do not give evidence that a god exists, or that God has given them direction for their thinking, emotions, moral standards and beliefs. In my research, I will examine two types of concepts, Secular concepts and Spiritual concepts. Secular concepts are a state of being separate from religion.[xiii] Spiritual concepts, deals with matters of the spirit, a concept closely tied to religious belief and faith, a transcendent reality.[xiv] These two types of concepts are what drive our communities today. The concepts can make the connection in defining the characteristics of the family, community and world.

Secular Concepts

In searching for various secular concepts, I discovered six classes that are identified in my research. Henry Clarence Thiessen defines the six classes that had their own world views. These are the views that an individual will usually accept when they are in need of fulfillment. They are the Atheistic view, Agnostic view, the Pantheistic view, the Polytheistic view, the Dualistic view, and the Deistic view.

Atheistic view is also known as "atheism". Atheism refers to a failure to recognize the only true God. Karen Armstrong writes that "During the sixteenth and seventeenth centuries, the word 'atheist' was still reserved exclusively for polemics.[xv] Polemics was similar to a journalist that practice disputing or arguing religious, philosophical, or political matters.[xvi] . Karen Armstrong further states that the term 'atheist' was an insult. Nobody would have dreamed of calling himself an atheist."[xvii] However in the 20th century, globalization and modernization contributed to the expansion of the term to refer to disbelief in all deities, though it remains common in Western society to describe atheism as simply "disbelief in God". My reading about atheism revealed the following three types. They are practical, dogmatic, and virtual atheism. Practical atheism is found among many people. "Many have rashly decided that all religion is phony" according to Henry Clarence Thiessen. Thiessen says "people like that are usually not confirmed atheists; they merely are indifferent to God. While perhaps acknowledging a God somewhere, they live and act as if there is no God to whom they are responsible."[xviii] As their religious interests are concerned, they are practical atheists". Dogmatic atheism is the type that atheist openly profess. This type of atheism has been revived in recent years. Thiessen points out that "communism openly professes itself to be atheistic and religion to be the opiate people."[xix] Thiessen says that, "virtual atheism is the kind that holds principles that are inconsistent with the belief of God or that define him in terms that do violence to the common usage of language". He further states that "most naturalists belong to these varieties". He shows the naturalists define God in such abstractions as "an active principle in nature," the social consciousness," "the unknowable," "personified reality," or "energy" are atheists of the second of these varieties." They are, in reality, doing violence to the established meaning of the term 'God.' Thiessen says, the "lifestyle of an atheist is seen as unsatisfactory, unstable, and arrogant. It is unsatisfactory because all atheists lack the assurance of the forgiveness of their sins. Their life is cold and empty, and they know nothing of peace with God. It is unstable because it is contrary to man's deepest convictions. Both Scripture and history shows that man necessarily and universally believes in the existence of God."

"The **Agonistic view** is sometimes applied to any doctrine that affirms the impossibility of any true knowledge, holding that all knowledge is relative and therefore uncertain. Some of these Agnostics were Greek Sophists and Skeptics as well as Aristole and Hume. The Agonistic position is highly unsatisfactory and unstable, and often displays a false humility. It suffers the same spiritual impoverishment as does the atheistic, but it is unsatisfactory also from the intelligent standpoint. Agnosticism proves this in it adoption of tentative views as working hypotheses".[xx]

The **Pantheistic view** states that all finite things are merely aspects, modifications, or parts of one eternal and self-existent being. It regards God as one with natural universe. God is all; all is God. It appears in a variety of forms today, some of them having in them also atheistic, polytheistic, or theistic elements. The pantheism usually looks upon their beliefs as a religion, bringing to them a kind of reverential submission. There are five leading types of pantheism. The Materialistic pantheism which holds that the 'matter" is the cause of all life and mind. Hylozoism and Panpsychism. These are the names from the same theory. There are, however, two types of this theory. The first holds that every particle of matter has, besides its physical properties, a principle of life. The second holds that mind and matter are distinct, but intimately and inseparably united. God in this view is the soul of the world. Then <u>Neutralism</u> which is a form of monism which holds that the ultimate reality is neither mind nor matter, but a neutral stuff of which mind and matter are but appearances or aspects.[xxi]

Baruch Spinoza in Thiessen book said that "there is but one substance with two attributes, thought and extension, or mind and matter, the totality of which is God. Idealism is the form of pantheism holds that ultimate reality is of the nature of mind and that the world is the product of mind, either of the individual mind or of the infinite mind. Last is the Philosophical mysticism which is a more absolute type of monism in existence. The mystic view the sense of otherness drops out altogether and the knower realizes that he is identical with the inner being of his subject. Just as we said in the beginning, some of the pantheistics are atheistic, polytheistic, or theistic elements in their theories. In conclusion, the Pantheistic view along with the five leading types of pantheism, destroy foundations of morals. They make all rational religion impossible, they deny personal and conscious immorality and they deify man by making him a part of God and last these views cannot account for concrete reality.[xxii]

Polytheism is the belief in or worship of multiple deities, such as gods and goddesses. These are usually assembled into a pantheon, along with their own mythologies and rituals. Many religions, both historical and contemporary, have a belief in polytheism, such as Hinduism, Shinto, Chinese folk religion, Neopagan faiths, Anglo-Saxon paganism and Greek paganism. [xxiii]

The **Dualistic view** assumes that there are two distinct and irreducible substances or principles. In Epistemology these are idea and object; in metaphysics, mind and matter; in ethics, good and evil; in religion, good or God, and evil or Satan.

The last is the **Deistic** view, which holds to the immanence of God to the exclusion of his transcendence. Deism holds to his transcendence to the exclusion of his immanence. For deism, God is present in creation only by his power, not in his very nature and being. Deism denies a special revelation, miracles, and providence. It claims that all truths about God are discoverable by reason and that the Bible is merely a book on the principles of natural religion, which are ascertainable by the light of nature.

With all the views researched you can understand how one can become who they are and how they established their individual lifestyle. All the different views have produced different culture throughout history. In a blog on Yahoo "Is reveling your atheism to others affects your work and your family relations?" there are a few people that express themselves about being atheist and their express their thoughts on their particular lifestyle. Superno writes, "I do not mention that I am an atheist or in any place where it is not relevant. Why would I? Many people have negative ideas about atheists so I try not to mention it, even if it comes up. I usually say something along the line of "I do not discuss religion" or "I do not believe in the supernatural," rarely an outright "I'm atheist." In fact, the only time I make my full views known is on Yahoo!" to answers and other similar debates. I do have very uptight Christian evangelicals on my mother's side who are very pushy and try to convert everyone. I've been told that birth control and even me dating Christians is against god. It has made relations with them difficult. Yet for all of the annoyances I face, it must be nothing compared to the poor atheist or non-believer who lives in a theocracy that legislates religion and imprisons/executes people for blasphemy and other solely religious crimes. Secularism protects people like me."

Mike Neckro writes "my work, no I don't think any of my CDs will ever be on the christian charts. Everyone in my family is an atheist. My life is good, except for every once in a while JWs or the

Mormons will slip through the radar. The fundies think of me as the devil." Sage wrote "Unlike Christians, Atheists have better manners and ethics than that - please do not ascribe your bad habits of pushing your views onto others!!!""

Notice the quandary with the views and blog comments, how they all talk about how good they live, cannot speak on their faith and hold in their thoughts. It shows how God is nowhere in their lives nor would they want Him to be there. This concept has brought our world in the same times as from the past. Nothing has changed as far as our belief system; however, these views give some people the idea that as long as I do my job, do not bother anyone and keep to myself, I will be fine. This doesn't answer the question of where to turn, when you don't know, where to turn? When man has failed himself, friends have failed you, the government dictates your life, belief, or turns you into a slave. Where do you turn then? Who can you call? This is a question that should rattle one's thought process. This should start your investigation of your concepts.

Spiritual Concepts

The spiritual concepts are concepts that are influenced by religion, or a faith based circle. The spiritual concept can be either a part of a particular religion or independent of religion, in a self directed and personal inner path. As part of a spiritual journey, spiritual concepts are usually descript and predictable, relating to one's personal relationship to God or a divine aspiration. Jolinda Cary gives an example of some spiritual concepts. Cary says "for a Christian, for example, spirituality involves developing a personal relationship and experience with Jesus Christ, likely through prayer, meditation or through selected activities (such as reading the Bible) in opposition to material gains and experiences. For the unaffiliated seeker, spirituality may be adapted and modeled after the sacred practices of a number of different religions or none at all. In either case spiritual matters are contrasted to the world of the senses and the needs of the human corporeal body and often involve an effort to reject, limit or transcend these senses and needs."[xxiv]

There are hundreds of religions today that are offered to the individual looking for a sense of attachment to a greater outside force other than them. I am going to cover six of the most popular religions and beliefs that are embraced from their religious concepts. Christianity, Islam, Judaism, Buddhism, Hinduism and Jainism are the most popular spiritual concepts people live by today.

Christianity is "a monotheistic religion [xxv] centered on the life and teachings of Jesus as presented in the New Testament Christians believe that, as the Messiah, Jesus was anointed by God as ruler and savior of humanity, and hold that Jesus' coming was the fulfillment of messianic prophecies of the Old Testament. The Christian concept of the Messiah differs significantly from the contemporary Jewish concept. The core concept of the Christian belief is that, through the death and resurrection of Jesus, sinful humans can be reconciled to God and thereby are offered salvation and the promise of eternal life.[xxvi]

Islam is a monotheistic, Abrahamic religion originating with the teachings of the Islamic prophet Muhammad, a 7th century Arab religious and political figure. Almost all Muslims belong to one of two major denominations, the Sunni or Shi'a. The Sunni concept of predestination is called divine decree,[xxvii] while the Shi'a version is called divine justice. In addition there are the Five Pillars in the Islamic law (sharia) which has developed a tradition of rulings that touch on virtually all aspects of life and society. This traditional concept encompasses everything from practical matters like dietary laws, banking to warfare and welfare. [xxviii]

Judaism is a monotheistic religion based upon conceptual principles and ethics embodied in the Hebrew Bible (Tanakh). According to Jewish tradition, Judaism begins with the Covenant between God and Abraham. Judaism is considered to be the first monotheistic religion. Many aspects of Judaism correspond to Western concepts of ethics and civil law. Judaism is among the oldest religious traditions still being practiced today, and many of its texts and traditions are central to other Abrahamic religions.[xxix]

Buddhism is a family of beliefs and practices widely considered to be a religion and is based on the teachings attributed to Siddhartha Gautama, commonly known as "The Buddha" (the Awakened One), who was born in what is today Nepal.[xxx]Followers of Buddha recognize him as an awakened teacher who shared his insights to help sentient beings end their suffering by understanding the true nature of phenomena, thereby escaping the cycle of suffering and rebirth, which is, achieving Nirvana. Among the concepts various schools of Buddhism apply towards their goals are: ethical conduct and altruistic behavior, devotional practices, ceremonies and the invocation of bodhisattvas, renunciation of worldly matters, meditation, physical exercises, study, and the cultivation of wisdom.[xxxi]

Hinduism is the predominant religion of the Indian subcontinent. Hinduism is often referred to as **Sanātana Dharma**, a Sanskrit phrase meaning "the eternal law", by its adherents.[xxxii] Hindu beliefs vary widely, with concepts of God and/or gods ranging from Panentheism, pantheism, monotheism, polytheism, and atheism with Vishnu and Shiva being the most popular deities. Other notable characteristics include a belief in reincarnation and karma, as well as personal duty, or dharma. Hinduism is the world's third largest religion after Christianity and Islam, with approximately a billion adherents, of whom about 905 million live in India.[xxxiii] Among its roots is the historical Vedic religion of Iron Age India, and as such Hinduism is often stated to be the "oldest religious tradition" or "oldest living major tradition." It is formed of diverse traditions and types and has no single founder.[xxxiv]

Jainism is one of the oldest religions that originated in India. The Jains concept, believe that every soul is divine and has the potential to achieve enlightenment or Moksha. Any soul which has conquered its own inner enemies and achieved the state of Supreme Being is called jina (Conqueror or Victor). Jainism is the path to achieve this state. Jainism is often referred to as Jain Dharma or Shraman Dharma or the religion of Nirgantha or religion of "Vratyas" by ancient texts. Jainism differs from other religions in its concept of God. Jainism regards every living soul as potentially divine. When the soul sheds its karmic bonds completely, it attains God-consciousness. It prescribes a path of non-violence to progress the soul to this ultimate goal. Jainism encourages spiritual development through reliance on and cultivation of one's own personal wisdom and self-control.[xxxv] The goal of Jainism is to realize the soul's true nature. First, in my study of secular and spiritual concepts I have discovered that they all have similar concepts and attributes. Both secular and spiritual concepts show the disciplines in each of their concepts. The ingredients of the two entities are the same, God, a god discipline, a text to follow and someone who poured the foundation into the secular or spiritual practice. An individual is always trying to fill a void, whether it is an empty soul or unhappiness. A concept must be followed either from secular concepts or spiritual concepts. The concept is what molds a person to the lifestyle they are going to live. My question is still the same. When the secular or spiritual concepts lead you to a dead end and you are about to give up what do you do? Where do you turn because you do not know? Second, since I am a Christian, I would say stay focused on what Jesus would do. Our economy is in the worst shape than ever before. Who would think, in 2009 we would be in a recession. People are living right now at the dead end. So after a careful observation of the secular and spiritual concepts, it shows we have to be disciplined, mature, surrendering, and have faith in our self and a higher authority.

Comparative Analysis (World Way vs. Gods Way)

Over a three day period, a team and I went out in the community and interviewed over 200 individuals. The interview was taken to identify people's way of living in the World's Way vs. Gods Way. This survey will reveal what concepts individuals choose to live by. Discovering one's concepts can better promote self-understanding, mutual understanding, as well as empathy and sensitivity with others, and real freedom for oneself in their direction for life. The survey identifies the secular and spiritual concepts that have characterized individuals. Most of the surveyors were professionals and blue collar workers. There were more female than males. The results were incorporated in the paper as well as the questions asked with the percentages of all the answers.

When asked the question,

1. Do you attend a religious service such as Church, Synagogue, Mosque etc?

   82% Always   8% Never   10% Sometimes

2. Do you attend interest groups such as PTA, Sororities, Fraternities, Country clubs,

   Community boards, Athletic teams or leisure activities?

Which group? _____

   Please respond about the group that is the most frequently attended.

   65% Always   3% Never   32% Sometimes

   3% Daily   70% Weekly   27% Monthly

3. Do you believe in GOD?

   98%Yes   92% No

4. Are you employed?

90% Yes   10% No

5. If you are employed do you call in sick when you have problems or your back is against the wall and you do not know where to turn?

5% Always   85% Never   10% Sometimes

6. Do you believe in successful people?

80% Always   5% Never   15% Sometimes

7. Do you believe in a Higher Power other than God? If so please explain.

3% Yes   97% No

_____

8. Do you go to the Bible when you have problems or your back is against the wall?

40% Always   5% Never   65% Sometimes

If not the Bible what guide sources do you go to_____

Majority was blank or referred to self help books.

9. Do you read self-help books when you have problems or your back is against the wall?

20% Always   8% Never   72% Sometimes

10. Do you go to your clergy when you have problems or your back is against the wall?

11% Always   25% Never   64% Sometimes

11. Do you go to a counselor/psychologist when you have problems or your back is against the wall?

7% Always   63% Never   30% Sometimes

12. Do you pray when you have problems or your back is against the wall?

20% Always   2% Never   88% Sometimes

13. When you have problems or your back is against the wall do you take matters into your own hands?

45% Always   5% Never   50% Sometimes

14. Have you ever asked for prayer when you are having problems or your back is against the wall?

62% Always   8% Never   30% Sometimes

15. Do you go shopping when you are having problems or your back is against the wall?

38% Always   45% Never   17% Sometimes

16. Do you get angry or upset when you are having problems or your back is against the wall and you don't know what to do?

76% Always   4% Never   20% Sometimes

17. When you do not know what to do, do you handle your problems by:

28% Expertise advice   55% Your own understanding 12% Clergy

5%   Wait till the last minute your direction

18. Do you have to be in control when you do not know what to do?

64% Always   6% Never   40% Sometimes

19. How do you make decisions when you do not know what to do?

84% Think things through   16% Just do it and worry about it later

20. Do you avoid difficult decisions that need to be made because you do not know?

79% Yes   21% No

21. Do you slow down think things through and act accordingly?

88% Yes   12% No

22. Do you do make decisions on your own through trial and error?

75% Yes   25% No

23. Do you think it is easier and more rewarding if you eliminate the guessing, trial and error, and misdirection and substitute it with proven techniques and approaches?

25% Always   9% Never   25% Sometimes

24. When you do not know where to turn, when you do not know where to go what do you do?

- Majority of the participants turn to prayer, parents, or a best friend when asked these questions.

- Women are significantly more likely than men to claim they need help in situations.

- Majority of participants believe in God however they do not turn to the Bible for life's instructions.

Why Not Trust Yourself

We all come to roads and periods in our lives when we don't know where to turn. We ponder on our options, and none of them feel quite right, or they have immense consequence that we are not yet willing to pay. It can leave us feel powerless, hopeless, and frightened, we may feel that we are alone and have to figure it out all alone. If we are in a dangerous situation, we must act, and act swiftly, in order to get out of danger. But let's suppose we are not faced with real danger, but a more expected intimidation; of the great unknown. This is the unknown of the potential, which never tells all, despite our best attempts at getting advice from our family, friends or ministers.

We may often feel in our hearts what is true and what is untrue, yet many of us do not listen to these inner messages. Instead, we put our trust in others, and then we feel betrayed when others let us down. When we choose to listen to and trust our own inner voice rather than give our power away to others, we will no longer put ourselves in positions to be used and betrayed.

Dr. Margaret Paul shares with us, if we promise ourselves that we will do something and then we don't do it, we are not being trustworthy with ourselves. Dr. Paul says "that this would be like promising a child something and then not doing it."[xxxvi] Eventually the child would learn not to trust you. The same applies with our inner child. If we promise ourselves; that is our inner self, that we will take care of ourselves in some way, and then we fail to do it, the inner self learns that there is no loving inner self to trust. Since many of us project onto secular or spiritual concepts of our own inner issues, it is likely that if we are not trustworthy with ourselves, then we will project untrustworthiness onto others. In other words, we will continue to distrust others as long as we are not behaving in a trustworthy way toward ourselves.

Since God gives us all free will, this says to me that God puts a lot of trust in us. God does not make us earn free will and then gives it to us. God just gives it to us with the confidence that we will make the right lifestyle choices. God put trust in Adam and Eve, but they are the ones who let God down. So, we must learn to trust ourselves because God does.

Your trust issues with yourself will be resolved when you develop a consistent Inner Bonding practice and learn to become a trustworthy adult with yourself, following through on what you say you will do and trusting your inner significant. You have to reprogram yourself, Proverbs 3:6-8 says, "In all thy ways acknowledge him, and he shall direct thy paths. Be not wise in thine own eyes: fear the LORD, and depart from evil. It shall be health to thy navel, and marrow to thy bones."[xxxvii] When you have the discipline to trust yourself you can have the discipline to lean not on your own understanding and acknowledge all your ways to God.

CHAPTER II

Realities of Acceptance Where You Are

With the present location in your life, you may be in an environment where things are not going the way you would like it. So, you ask yourself the question, where do you turn from here? By now, you have figured out that the concepts you live by works only to a certain degree. Furthermore the situation seems damaging to your lifestyle, your spirituality, and conscience. The biggest challenge of all time is to face the reality in the present moment. You can start asking yourself questions 'where did I go wrong from here? Did I really listen? Am I blaming others for my situation? When facing your problem the self help concept wants to manifest itself. The flesh wants to allow the environmental concepts to take over the mind and control our emotions to handle the reality. The reality only needs a focus point. It seems the reality is unconquerable. The reality is that it is going to take something supernatural to supersede the reality. That supernatural ability is utilized as you accept where you are. Face the reality and do what you are not comfortable doing. Trusting yourself, to trust God, in a way you have never done before. That will be the supernatural for yourself, because you have never relied on God and scripture only.

Present Location of Reality

In our churches today, we often see ourselves facing realities of failed marriages, job loss, death etc. In church, church groups or Bible studies, we all want to make a change. However the church model is, the traditions and the reality is, it seems like there won't be any change. Paul D. Meier asks, "are we immature about the situation, or could we handle it maturely?" with regards to an unhappy marriage facing an unhappy reality. Gene Mims, the author of Kingdom Focused Church, addresses the issue of an unhappy minister. The minister has been contracted to a new position as senior pastor and now feels if he is at the perfect church. What a time to be asking himself now. The author writes how all churches are imperfect. Mims gives the reality direction as he says "the only church you can change is the one you're serving in right now." Mims further states that you have to avoid the temptation to say," You know, the church is supposed to be ...." Or "I need to be in a church that ....".[xxxviii] As Mims thought, like the majority of us, that church is a place where we all get along. We can see the present location is the best place to accept the reality of where we are. The best thing we can do as Mims says, "Be the best because God gives everyone a different set of tools to work with."

Notice Location Where You Are (Environment Awareness)

On a compass, you can tell which direction you are traveling by four points, north, east, south, and west. Which direction are you going to take? Which turn is the correct turn for you? Dr. Ed Wheat, a marriage counselor states in his book "Love Life For Every Married Couple", a Christian psychiatrist Paul D. Meier, is quoted as saying, "there are only three choices for any person involved in an unhappy marriage; (1) get a divorce- the greatest cop-out and by far the most immature choice; (2) tough out the marriage without working to improve it- another immature decision but not quite as irresponsible as divorce; and (3) maturely face up to personal hang-ups and choose to build an intimate marriage out of the existing one-the only really mature choice to make."[xxxix] After reading his recommendations I saw a great illustration on handling realities. I saw how I handle present and past realities. I stated earlier how I had my own concepts and they lead me to a dead end. My current concept is a supernatural concept. The concept is sticking to the basics, doing things Gods way, relying on scripture and God. You may be in the position you are in because of your environment. In most instances I have witnessed, people are in negative situations because their family and friends are not part of healthy and positive environments. Most of our family and friends are in unhealthy environments and negative situations. Just remember no one is perfect, but be careful, as the old saying goes "Misery loves Company". Proverbs illustrates the type of environment you could possibly be in. Proverbs shows you where you are, where you are heading and how you can depart from it. I remember how I always wanted to be a part of the esteemed, entrepreneurs in my city. I thought I made it; I had political power, financial power, and spiritual power and I was a part of the elite class. The indulgence of the power, money, and material possessions painted a picture of me in the world as Prince charming. Though I had power, affluence, and more possessions than you could imagine, my attitude was awful and anything less than charming. I was ruthless, heartless, selfish and mean. All I cared about was myself and felt everyone owed me something. The spiritual power I had I used for myself, never to help others. This environment I was living in seemed to be great, money, cars, clothes, jewelry, home theater, were all blessings from Satan, which I misunderstood as blessings from God. In the flesh, a love for self satisfaction is always brewing. You can be a person of faith or a person of the world. It doesn't matter. Self satisfaction is something that has to be restrained. Furthermore, when you experiment with lust, that is a self satisfaction, you just created a recipe for disaster. A person in the worldly environment is always looking for the next moment. If they have a hunger for self-satisfaction; they will do anything to get it, pay attention to your location before it is too late. The secular books I was reading would only take me so far, the business circles only took me so far, my church could only take me so far, money in the bank could only take me so far. I would be in a place of relaxation, but when the spa time was complete the realities were waiting on the other side.

During a period of time when my marriage was failing, I needed a change of environment; the worldly environment had taken its toll. My environment needed to change; I remember the change like it was yesterday. I met a member of my church for lunch to talk about my career change; I figured if I just got a job in pharmaceutical sales and attend church regularly with my ministerial duties that would be enough. The luncheon took place at the Bread of Heaven in Alcoa, Tennessee. Todd Kelly, a former super bowl champion and a deacon at our church, was a medical device sales representative who I thought could help me launch my pharmaceutical sales career. At the luncheon, during the first five to seven minutes Todd told me I would make plenty of money, where to develop the best resume and where to get started. Then, in the next sixty minutes the conversation turned to visiting a Proverbs men class with him on Tuesdays. This was an environmental location that I did not think would help me. However, I went the next week just to return the favor of meeting Todd. When I attended the bible study group, I noticed an unusual environmental awareness; I was introduced to the study of the book of Proverbs with men that were hungry for another kind of direction. The scriptures from Proverbs showed me my present location. After I noticed my location, the scriptures of Proverbs showed me how to accept the realities, then the scriptures of Proverbs showed me how to notice the location where I was going. Most of the time, we face reality immaturely, just as Paul D. Meier says, about an unhappy marriage facing an unhappy reality. Marriage is not the problem; the individuals in the marriage are the problem. The workplace is not the problem the individual or co-workers are the problem. The church is not the problem the individual church member is the problem. If we can slow down, and look at our present location we can use GPS to find our way. But we have to accept our location to move on.

Accept Location

The present location God has for you may be the church van driver. For me, it is Sunday school. Clarence Swarenger and I were put to the task of creating a new College Sunday school class. The task was not a problem. The situation was, there were no college students, except for those students home for the summer. These students would be going back to school in three weeks. In the beginning, the class went well and Clarence and I did all we could do. We then opened the class for anyone that was interested. People started to come and when the book study ended, the class fell apart. The reality was that the class seemed to be over. The Sunday school board was asking how they could help. The senior Pastor was trying to make sure Clarence and I was doing what we needed to do. The reality was that it appeared to be a failure and all eyes were on the Sunday school teacher who never had focus.

From my reading the Kingdom Focused Church and I as reflect on it now, Clarence and I were totally off focused. Mims says " if you want to grow a church, you must either start something new, like new ministries or worship services, or multiply what you currently do"[xl] The fact was something new was created, however step three was missing under the Multiplying for Kingdom Effectiveness: Train, train, train. There were gaps due to miscommunication and often we would not have class at all. Clarence and I had to face the reality of what had happened and regroup. The church was so concerned with the numbers and our recruitment strategies, which it failed just as it was set up. So Clarence and I had to remember who we were teaching the class for. Clarence said it was not for the church, not for the Sunday school board or the senior pastor. It was for the main target, God. By Gods grace, I was taking the course Mission of the church. We restarted the class being Kingdom focused and followed it step by step with one prospect. Clarence said he had to accept the reality that the class fell apart. However, it was not Kingdom focused. It was focused on numbers and bodies.

The one person he had to teach in the Sunday school class was the one that needed the attention from God. The person he was teaching was leaving the Muslim faith, and he needed that one-on-one attention at the time. When Clarence and I look back we were not Kingdom Focused. Mims says about declining churches, is all about focus "I believe the problem is focus. If we lack a kingdom focus in our work, it shows up everywhere."[xli] So, now our Sunday school class is growing more than expected. Mims was right the Kingdom focus showed up.

You Can Make a Difference

By making small positive changes into your lifestyle you can make a big difference to your well-being, health and how you feel when you do not know where to turn. Your new understanding, GPS, concepts, trusting yourself, and maturity of facing reality can make a difference.

To help you make those lasting lifestyle changes, you can use the following concepts from scripture and following your fathers coordinates including submitting to your father, moving toward the light, disciplining yourself, love while traveling, living in peace and enjoying the ride.

Your personal invitation and activity is tailored to suit you and designed specifically to help you find simple and manageable ways to lead a rejuvenated life. We have to detoxify from the materialism of the world. We must die to self. When the difference is made others will want the same joy.

CHAPTER III

Submit Yourself to Your Father

The intent of this chapter is to explore the steps that start the transition of total submission to the direction from the life setbacks, disappointments and challenges. Life has just kicked you in the rear, some peace needs to be found, you may not like it, but you need to get through it. We all have questions that we want to eliminate confusion. Some way, somehow, can the struggle of life be lived a little more peacefully? The questions of why God has put me in the position? What lesson can I learn from this? Why trust an unknown Father in uncertain times. How submission will give endurance in uncertain times. These are the things that will be discussed in this chapter.

While growing up there were very few fathers in households in my neighborhood, including mine. My mother raised me with the help of my grandparents, aunt and uncle. A two parent household while I was growing up consisted of a child and his/her mother. My father was never around while I was growing up. One day, while I was sitting in class I figured out my father's actions. I have a half-brother and half-sister and all of us are a month apart. That means that my father was going from house to house daily. I used to hear mothers in my neighborhood say to their children every time their son or daughter got into trouble " you are going to be just like your father" even though the mothers were really saying do not be like your father. That was one statement I was going to make sure I was not going fall into, being, like my father. I did all in my power not to have children months apart. I now have two daughters that are by my wife Heather. In my mind I never thought about having a father around. When I was in the fifth grade my father ended his life, so I had to never submit to a father in my household. I never had to submit to my father outside the household. My grandfather and my Aunt Carolyn's husband, Uncle Nathaniel were the only men in my life, each man gave me character in life. My grandfather, Big John Nash gave me the relationship skills in having partnerships. Uncle Nathaniel introduced me to fashion and automobiles. Those skills took me a long way, even today I live by those skills. I submitted to concepts from those men, but never submitted to the men themselves. However, the submission to the concepts only took me so far. I never had a father to look up to so I adopted my own father figure concepts from Uncle Nathaniel and my Grandfather Big John Nash. Through the times, I needed a father I never made an excuse. I would accept responsibility and take whatever came my way. Sometimes situations were tougher than others, but submission was never a tool to use. Submission from a man's point of view means weak, incapable, fearful, underdeveloped, or powerless. One day God was calling me to come home and do his will. Like most, I answered when I wanted to. God said "I want you to start doing my will now" I said back to God "When I finish this deal for this new Real Estate office I will do whatever," then God sent a friend my minister friend, Eric Bonner with a new appointment at a church. Every time Eric asked me to meet with him, I would put him off. Basically I was lying. I did not want to be a part of any church activities. I wanted to do real estate ventures. I put him off on three different occasions. Every time I said I was busy and had to be somewhere. I would end up running into Eric and how uncomfortable that was!

In the days to come I was supposed to close on my loan for my new real estate office. God said "are you going to do what I am saying to do?" My response was the same. "When I finish this deal for this new real estate office I will do whatever". Now this was the second time God had called me and I ignored Him, both times I said no to God. The bank called and put off my loan, I had some closings that were delayed as well. The third time I was contacted by the bank, it was a call stating the Vice President I was working with no longer worked for the bank. They did not even know where he went. I went to the bank the next day and the new Vice President said to me "I know you think I am the devil, but I am not, however I can't fund the loan". The same day, I received a utility bill for four thousand dollars. The building I was going to make my new real estate office had been burglarized for the copper plumbing. The water had been running for about two to three weeks. Then God said to me "are you going to listen now?" I said to God "I am going to write a business plan and get an empowerment zone grant and finish my goal" The next couple of days I went to write my grant and a lady from my church was working in the empowerment zone office. I just knew I was going to get the grant now. Mrs. Jackie Robinson helped me with all the applications and my day started off good. The next day Mrs.

Robinson was no longer working at the empowerment zone office, I sat in the empowerment zones computer lab and began writing. Out of six hours I had only typed two lines, it seemed like my hand was filled with lead, I could not write, I could not move. I planned to return the next day. The next day the same thing happened, two lines and heaviness. That day it seemed like I had wrestled with a bear, I was exhausted. Then I sat back and thought what was going on. I saw God was trying to tell me something, but I was ignoring Him. I was arrogant and ignorant, I had a father that wanted me to come home. So, that day I sat in the computer lab chair and said to God, "Father I surrender to you, Father I submit to you, Father I am all yours, I will do whatever you want me to do". Then as soon as I finished speaking, my friend Eric called me on the cell phone and said something told me to call you, I told him the good news, I apologized to him, and we met the next hour. When I left Eric that day, I went to pray on the office building to be sold, it seemed like the weight of the world was off my shoulders. We think because our birth father is not around we don't have a father. You have a father, you may not be able to see, touch or feel God, but he is your Father that breath of life into your lungs. God is the best father I could ever have. Submit to God, honor him as your father and follow the coordinates.

Follow the Coordinates

When you submit to God, He will supply all your needs. When I answered my call to the ministry, I prayed on the office building I talked about earlier. By following God's coordinates, He answered my prayer the next day. A contract cash offer came for the office building for the exact amount I had wanted the building for including the portion for the utility bill. Every since then I have been sold out for God, God calls us, but we ignore. The more I submit to God, the clearer the path is to follow. Dr. Gregory Frizzel states "for all believers, there will be many points we must choose Gods will and way over our own (Isaiah 55:8). Our flesh and natural desires may clamor for one course of action, yet we know Gods wills another. Only as you choose to deny self, and by faith obey God, will you know His glorious power."[xlii]

When a child is in the kitchen they will always go for the snacks, junk foods or sodas, the healthy coordinates are rarely chosen. The same in life, we always want to go after lust, desire, disobedience, or short cuts. Following the coordinates seems difficult when there is no discipline.

King Solomon was made King by God. The King was young and he knew he wanted to follow in his father's footsteps. Solomon loved God and went to the highest places to burnt offerings in honor of God. Solomon had a Kingship, but he did not have a heart to lead Gods people. In a dream God spoke to Solomon and said "Solomon, ask for anything you want me to give you." In the Dream Solomon replied, "You have been very kind to my father, your servant. That's because he was faithful to you. He did what was right and his heart was honest. And you have continued to be very kind to him. You have given him a son to sit on his throne this very day. Now, O LORD my God, you have made your servant king in place of my father David. But I am only a little child and do not know how to carry out my duties. Your servant is here among the people you have chosen, a great people, too numerous to count or number. So give your servant a discerning heart to govern your people and to distinguish between right and wrong. For who is able to govern this great people of yours?" I Kings 3: 6-9

The Lord was pleased that Solomon had asked for this. So God said to him, "Since you have asked for this and not for long life or wealth for yourself, nor have asked for the death of your enemies but for discernment in administering justice, I will do what you have asked. I will give you a wise and discerning heart, so that there will never have been anyone like you, nor will there ever be. Moreover, I will give you what you have not asked for—both riches and honor—so that in your lifetime you will have no equal among kings. And if you walk in my ways and obey my statutes and commands as David your father did, I will give you a long life."[xliii] Solomon knew he was not knowledgeable enough to carry to the mission as a King. Solomon lived where he saw his father follow the coordinates of God. So, when he was asked by God "What can He give" Solomon, asked for coordinates to be able to judge from right and wrong. God answered the request and Solomon followed the coordinates until he let his own will deceive him. In the Old Testament, God sent people to deliver His message to do His will. In the New Testament, God sent a personal messenger his only begotten son Jesus. Jesus followed the coordinates of God. Jesus was an example for us to follow for God's will.

Jesus Coordinates

The following Scriptures show that God became man, "the Word became flesh".[xliv] Jesus came in order to authenticate the promises made to the fathers and to show mercy to the Gentiles. There's the incredibly challenging standard of living like Jesus in every way, of devoting ourselves to being like Jesus, to living as Jesus. It's a challenge for the best of the best! But Jesus thinks we can do it! Jesus offers us to follow him, to take his yoke, to follow his way of life. Love and trust will compel you to deny you're very self, to crucify your flesh, your very person, and to attack the hordes of hell on behalf of Jesus and His little ones. You will never crucify your flesh out of guilt, or in obedience to rules, or because of a promised reward. Love alone will get you there. God is calling each of us to move past the lesser reasons for following Him. He's calling us into the highest of reasons, love for Jesus. Can you follow the coordinates? Jesus said," Whoever follows me will never walk in darkness" (John 8:12)[xlv]

The cross lies at the heart of all God did through Jesus Christ. It is the supreme example of God's power and wisdom displayed in what the world considers weakness and foolishness (1 Corinthians

1:18-25).[xlvi] And anyone who wants to know God must find Him in Christ crucified. But the cross is as central to following Christ daily as it is to knowing Him initially. Notice the word *daily* in the invitation of Jesus: "Then He said to them all, 'If anyone desires to come after Me, let him deny himself, and take up his cross daily, and follow Me'" (Luke 9:23)[xlvii]. As Jesus was willing to go to the cross to do the will of the Father (Philippians 2:8), so we must be willing to follow Jesus to the cross, daily denying any desires that conflict with His so that we may daily live for Him. While we may truly speak of glory inaugurated by the resurrection and ascension of Jesus, identifying with following Him in this world involves suffering.[xlviii]

Coordinates of the Disciples

Traveling can sap your strength and your sanity. You can't control check-in lines, flight delays or the behavior of a frisky child in the seat behind you, but you can eliminate a multitude of problems by incorporating ideas into your pre-trip planning. You probably would collect information, as soon as you decide to make a trip. You would gather contact names, airline tickets, hotel and car rental confirmations, maps and driving directions, and receipts. However, in order to gather the information you would have to have some kind of knowledge you have been taught. The disciples were taught about travel. I don't mean the travel vacation; I am talking about the travel for their spiritual journey.

What is a Disciple? A disciple is a pupil or student that was chosen to follow Jesus and to listen to his teaching. The twelve disciples were followers of Jesus whom he had chosen to become his core group, the people he talked things over with and depended on.

Jesus taught his followers to make the pursuit of the Kingdom of God their highest priority (Matt 6:33). Discipleship is a life-style which first seeks the kingdom and its justice, Jesus wherever he goes and was willing to renounce all other interests to the extent that they become obstacles to the goals. That essential discipline was probably necessary to overcome the exaggerated family loyalty common in the Levant, and to insure the freedom for a life of itinerant preaching. It is also an application of the command to love God with one's whole heart, soul and might (Deut 6:5), interpreted in such a way that heart means all one's affective faculties, soul means life (to the point of martyrdom), and might means material possessions. Thus discipleship is a radical form of love.

Sightseeing

When you plan for your visit to the Grand Canyon you may want to get information from the National Park Service website and the Grand Canyon Chamber of Commerce website for directions and needed supplies. The travel website literature and maps may help you see the Grand Canyon layout. While traveling you may want to stop by a visitor's center once you arrive at the Grand Canyon. While driving your car to the Grand Canyon, you see several parts and scenic spots, desert view, and places to eat. While being absorb in the distractions you have lost the since of direction. The road signs are showing different directions and locations. The distractions you have gazed at have caused you to become lost. In today's world, it is easy to get distracted. In fact, distractions are the cause of most accidents. What about our spiritual life? Can distractions get in the way there as well? How many times have we been driving down the road, possibly talking to the other person in the car, listening to the radio or just looking at scenery, when suddenly you realize you missed your exit? This is a classic example of being distracted. If this hasn't happened to you so far, don't worry; it wills one day if you keep looking off the road.

What is a distraction? Webster's defines distraction as follows: **Distraction** :Dis-'trac-tion, **1.** The act of distracting; a drawing apart; separation. To create distraction's among us. **2.** That which diverts attention; a diversion. "Domestic distractions." G. Eliot. **3.** A diversity of direction; detachment. [xlix]

Concupiscence, is another term used as desire, the KJV translation of Greek epithumia, "desire, lust." The Greeks used the term to mean excitement about something in a neutral sense and then in an evil sense of wrongly valuing earthly things. The New Testament knows desire can be good (Matthew 13:17; Luke 22:15; Philippians 1:23; 1 Thessalonians 2:17). In fact, the New Testament uses the verb form more often in a good sense than in a bad.

The bad sense of epithumia is desire controlled by sin and worldly instincts rather than by the Spirit (Galatians 5:16). Everyone has been controlled by such desires before their commitment to Christ (Ephesians 2:3; Titus 3:3). Such desire is part of the old life without

Christ and is deceitful (Ephesians 4:22). Such desire can be for sex (Matthew 5:28), material goods (Mark 4:19), riches (1 Timothy 6:9), and drunkenness (1 Peter 4:3). The Christian life then is a war between desires of the old life and desire to follow the Spirit (Galatians 5:15-24; 1 Peter 2:11), the Spirit-led life crucifying worldly desires (Galatians 5:24). (Note the list of fleshly desires in (Galatians 5:19-21.) As the new life comes through the Spirit, so old desires come through Satan (John 8:44) and the world of which he is prince (1 John 2:16). Such desires can make slaves of people (2 Peter 2:18-20). Desire brings temptation, leading to sin, resulting in death (James 1:14-15). People cannot blame God, for He allows them freedom to choose and gives them over to what they choose (Romans 1:24). God did give the law which defined wrong desires as concupiscence or sin. The power of sin then changed the good commandment into an instrument to arouse human desires to experience new arenas of life. Thus they sin and die rather than trust God's guidance through the law that such arenas are outside God's plan for life and thus should not be experienced (Romans 7:7-8). Either sin brings death, or believers in Christ murder evil lusts (Colossians 3:5).

In a very limited sphere of life, Paul called on believers to rise above the normal activities caused by lust in society. He called on faithfulness in marriage rather than on the immoral practices of the Greek and Roman world of his day (1 Thessalonians 4:4-5).[l]

 As God's people, we have a responsibility to be good examples to those around us. If we lose sight of this responsibility even for a flash, split second, or moment we are in jeopardy of having a spiritual accident. There are not any statistics for the leading cause of our spiritual accidents, but I would venture to say that, much like car accidents, it would be distractions. Are we focused on the Kingdom and God's plan, or do we get sidetracked and become angry just like the world around us? It's human nature to retaliate when someone hurts us, but is that what we should do? [li]

Hebrews 12:1-2 says we must focus on Jesus: "Therefore we also, since we are surrounded by so great a cloud of witnesses, let us lay aside every weight, and the sin which so easily ensnares us, and let us run with endurance the race that is set before us, looking unto Jesus, the author and finisher of our faith, who for the joy that was set before Him endured the cross, despising the shame, and has sat down at the right hand of the throne of God."[lii]

And I Corinthians 7:35 says, "And this I say for your own profit, not that I may put a leash on you, but for what is proper, and that you may serve the Lord without distraction." The interesting thing about distractions is that when they happen, we are totally unaware. We have no idea that anything at all is happening to us, and we simply react.[liii] Psalm 86:11: "Teach me Your way, O LORD; I will walk in Your truth; unite my heart to fear Your name." Romans 12:17: "Repay no one evil for evil. Have regard for good things in the sight of all men." Colossians 3:1-2: "If then you were raised with Christ, seek those things which are above, where Christ is sitting at the right hand of God. Set your mind on things above, not on things on the earth." Also in I Timothy 4:16 we are told to "focus on your life and your teaching" (God's Word).

While it is almost unavoidable that we will become distracted in life, it is most important that we bear in mind to stay focused on God and His ways. We learn to continue and enhance our studying in God's Word and praying for His guidance. We then put into action the teachings by following His Word and, every time achievable, steering clear of the areas and ways that lead us to distraction. It's not always easy, but we can have God's help.

Desires

There is always something that pulls us into a situation that is not in our lane of life. The bill boards on the highways have attractive signage that lures us in. There are flashing lights, neon lights, and items hanging off the bill boards to draw us into their establishments. Somehow the advertisements bonds with our intellect, then our curiosity leads to our emotion. Our emotions heat up a little more than the last expedition. Then little by little we keep inching into the shadows. The desires are flames that need to be tamed. So what is desire? To express a wish for : REQUEST, to express a wish to : ASK, obsolete :Invite. Desire stresses the strength of feeling and often implies strong intention or aim.[liv] Is it God's desire for all men to be saved? "…This is good and acceptable in the sight of God our Savior, who desires all men to be saved and to come to the knowledge of the truth." - 1 Tim 2: 3, 4. If God desires that all men be saved, but does man want to desire to be of God or mans will. There is in reality very little that we can get through our own power, but this is, of course, where surrender comes in. It is clear, that God desires all men to obey His commands whether they are degenerate or not, and this includes the command to believe. God holds all of us responsible for not obeying. In other words, God desires that all men come to faith. God commands all men everywhere to repent and His commandment is to believe in the Lord Jesus Christ. Then there is no other possible conclusion than to say God desires all men, elect and reprobate, to obey His commands, including the command to believe the gospel. John Hendry says, that when Jesus went into Jerusalem and saw the Israelites, they reject Him. Jesus said:

" Jerusalem, Jerusalem, who kills the prophets and stones those who are sent to her! How often I wanted to gather your children together, the way a hen gathers her chicks under her wings, and you were unwilling." Matt 23:37

Jesus truly mourns over people who are unwilling to come to Him; even the degenerate. He yearns for them to come and holds out His hands to them but they are obstinate and will not come simply because they don't want to come. He desires that these persons be saved in the sense that He wants them to believe in Him. But they love their sin more than they love their God. This is the natural condition of all men apart from God's grace. So he desires all men to believe, but he saves only those who He sovereignty sets His affection upon, according to the good pleasure of His will. His reasons for choosing some and not others have not been revealed to us. This is part of His secret counsel or decretive will. But rest assured that God will act according to His perfections and conspire with His wisdom to do what is right. There is, in fact, no better reason in the universe than God wills something to take place.

The gospel is declared to all men ... it is news for all to hear, but, due to our natural rebellion and hatred of God, all men reject God. Therefore since men are never found naturally willing to submit in faith to the humbling terms of the gospel of Christ, men will not come into the light (John 14:17; John 10:26; John 6:44; John 3:20; Rom 3:11). But thanks be to God, who is yet merciful, coming to those He has chosen from eternity giving them eternal life. What they could not do for themselves, He mercifully does for them. Those who "have ears to hear" are the same as those whom God's favor rests. So even, the desire for belief itself, like all spiritual blessings, was purchased by Christ on the cross.[lv]

Carrying The Cross

The desires we have for the world like wanting that new car, house, job, knowledge to become successful, how to control others, control self, become rich are desires that drive us every time to a dead-end when they are fulfilled. After having all those things we then become bored with them. The desire flame was not the same flame as before. Jesus says, in Matthew 16:24 to the disciples that "If anyone would come after me, he must deny himself and take up his cross and follow me." Somehow, we must understand that we must carry our own cross. However, we must put our own desires in Gods hand and carry out his mission. He will carry out the desires of our heart. Carrying the cross is something we need to do with joy and delight, not filled with misery and unconscious feelings. A majority of us are uncomfortable to dying to self because we have been conditioned to feed ourselves to the American dream. However it is something we are afraid of. When you surrender to share responsibly the weight is much lighter. When you only carry your cross and leave your desires behind the load is lighter. Jesus has already carried the load. While carrying the cross *we* need to repent. The Bible tells us to "repent and turn to God" (Acts

26:20b). It is not something that we should wait for God to do for us. Jesus told us an important command in the Bible that says, "...The Lord our God is one Lord; and you shall love the Lord your God with all your heart, and with all your soul, and with your entire mind, and with all your strength" (Mark 12:29-30).

We Christians know we should love God, but it is up to us that we carry the cross, the Bible says,

"But I have this against you, that you have left your first love. Therefore remember from where you have fallen, and repent and do the deeds you did at first..." (Rev. 2:4,5). Repentance is very important for our salvation. But repentance is also important for those of us who have already chosen to follow God. We need to repent because we have left our first love for God and have fallen in first love with our earthly materials, ways understanding.

The Bible says, "Repent and turn away from your idols and turn your faces away from all your abominations." (Eze. 14:6). Another text in the Bible says, "return to the Lord with all your heart, remove the foreign gods...from among you and direct your hearts to the Lord and serve Him alone; and He will deliver you..." (1 Sam. 7:3).

Directing your heart toward God should be at the very aim of how you live your Christian lifestyle. The Lord is our shepherd, however

He will allow us to wander if we so choose, even though it hurts Him to see it happen.

The Scriptures says to, "...train yourself to be godly" (1 Tim. 4:7 NIV). It instructs *us* to, "...sanctify Christ as Lord in your hearts" (1 Pet. 3:15a). It is imperative that we take action to direct our desire back to God and away from earthly concepts.

Directing your heart toward God is all about "dying to self." Jesus told us, "Whoever does not carry his own cross and come after Me cannot be My disciple" (Luke 14:27). Repentance and turning to God is not an option. Because our hearts are so prone to wander, we individuals must continue directing our heart toward God and it must become a natural part of everyday lifestyle.

The apostle Paul wrote, "Always carrying about in the body the dying of Jesus, so that the life of Jesus also may be manifested in our body" (2 Cor. 4:10). Paul shows repentance is not an end in itself. The reason is so that the "life of Jesus" can be manifested.

We must not wait for God to do our repenting for you and I. God is waiting for us! The Bible says,

"and My people who are called by My name humble themselves and pray and seek My face and turn from their wicked ways, then I will hear from heaven, will forgive their sin and will heal their land." (2 Chron. 7:14).

The settlement will be great when God's people on an extensive scale repent and turn to God. But since God has told us so clearly that we should be the ones to turn our heart toward Him, we can be confident that the Bible also tells us how. It is time to take action and carry your cross.   (Please Continue to Volume 2)

If You Enjoyed the Book Please Continue to Volume II
(Volume II contains the last four chapters)

Where to Turn

When You Don't Know Where to Turn

In Modern Times

Volume II

Thanks for Reading

Marcus

www.marcusblakemore.com

My Questions and Your Answers

The last portion of this book is devoted to a series of questions for your review and reflection. Please feel free to use it to jot down your thoughts and pensive considerations.

My prayers are with you as you are moving through to greater insight into God's matchless plan for your life!

God's GPS is His way of guiding us. In what instances have you
recently ignored God's GPS? What were the results or final
outcome?

_____

_____

_____

_____

_____

_____

_____

_____

_____

_____

_____

_____

_____

_____

_____

_____

_____

_____

_____

_____

_____

_____

_____

_____

_____

_____

_____

_____

_____

_____

_____

_____

_____

_____

God's GPS is His way of guiding us. In what instances have you recently ignored God's GPS? What were the results or final outcome?

_____

_____

_____

_____

_____

_____

_____

_____

_____

_____

_____

_____

_____

_____

_____

_____

_____

_____

_____

_____

_____

_____

_____

_____

_____

_____

_____

_____

_____

_____

_____

_____

_____

_____

_____

God's GPS is His way of guiding us. In what instances have you recently ignored God's GPS? What were the results or final outcome?

_____
_____
_____
_____
_____
_____
_____
_____
_____
_____
_____
_____
_____
_____
_____
_____
_____
_____
_____
_____
_____
_____
_____
_____
_____
_____
_____
_____
_____
_____
_____
_____
_____
_____
_____
_____
_____

God's GPS is His way of guiding us. In what instances have you recently ignored God's GPS? What were the results or final outcome?

_____
_____
_____
_____
_____
_____
_____
_____
_____
_____
_____
_____
_____
_____
_____
_____
_____
_____
_____
_____
_____
_____
_____
_____
_____
_____
_____
_____
_____
_____
_____
_____
_____
_____
_____

Discuss reasons why you feel (or don't feel), the Bible is the best resource for direction in life? List some scenarios where you have consulted the Bible and found answers. List those where you did not find your answer there.

Discuss reasons why you feel (or don't feel), the Bible is the best resource for direction in life? List some scenarios where you have consulted the Bible and found answers. List those where you did not find your answer there.

_____

_____

_____

_____

_____

_____

_____

_____

_____

_____

_____

_____

_____

_____

_____

_____

_____

_____

_____

_____

_____

_____

_____

_____

_____

_____

_____

_____

_____

_____

_____

_____

_____

_____

_____

_____

_____

_____

_____

_____

_____

Discuss reasons why you feel (or don't feel), the Bible is the best resource for direction in life? List some scenarios where you have consulted the Bible and found answers. List those where you did not find your answer there.

Discuss reasons why you feel (or don't feel), the Bible is the best resource for direction in life? List some scenarios where you have consulted the Bible and found answers. List those where you did not find your answer there.

_____
_____
_____
_____
_____
_____
_____
_____
_____
_____
_____
_____
_____
_____
_____
_____
_____
_____
_____
_____
_____
_____
_____
_____
_____
_____
_____
_____
_____
_____
_____
_____
_____

Discuss reasons why you feel (or don't feel), the Bible is the best resource for direction in life? List some scenarios where you have consulted the Bible and found answers. List those where you did not find your answer there.

_____

_____

_____

_____

_____

_____

_____

_____

_____

_____

_____

_____

_____

_____

_____

_____

_____

_____

_____

_____

_____

_____

_____

_____

_____

_____

_____

_____

_____

_____

_____

_____

_____

_____

_____

_____

_____

_____

Discuss reasons why you feel (or don't feel), the Bible is the best resource for direction in life? List some scenarios where you have consulted the Bible and found answers. List those where you did not find your answer there.

_____
_____
_____
_____
_____
_____
_____
_____
_____
_____
_____
_____
_____
_____
_____
_____
_____
_____
_____
_____
_____
_____
_____
_____
_____
_____
_____
_____
_____
_____
_____
_____
_____
_____
_____
_____

How important is it necessary for you, personally to pray, and ask for others to pray, when you are facing difficulties?

_____
_____
_____
_____
_____
_____
_____
_____
_____
_____
_____
_____
_____
_____
_____
_____
_____
_____
_____
_____
_____
_____
_____
_____
_____
_____
_____
_____
_____
_____
_____
_____
_____
_____
_____
_____
_____
_____

How important is it necessary for you, personally to pray, and ask for others to pray, when you are facing difficulties?

How important is it necessary for you, personally to pray, and ask for others to pray, when you are facing difficulties?

_____
_____
_____
_____
_____
_____
_____
_____
_____
_____
_____
_____
_____
_____
_____
_____
_____
_____
_____
_____
_____
_____
_____
_____
_____
_____
_____
_____
_____
_____
_____
_____
_____

How important is it necessary for you, personally to pray, and ask for others to pray, when you are facing difficulties?

_____

_____

_____

_____

_____

_____

_____

_____

_____

_____

_____

_____

_____

_____

_____

_____

_____

_____

_____

_____

_____

_____

_____

_____

_____

_____

_____

_____

_____

_____

_____

_____

_____

How helpful do you find self-help tools to be in your life?

_____
_____
_____
_____
_____
_____
_____
_____
_____
_____
_____
_____
_____
_____
_____
_____
_____
_____
_____
_____
_____
_____
_____
_____
_____
_____
_____
_____
_____
_____
_____
_____
_____
_____

How helpful do you find self-help tools to be in your life?

How important is it for you to be in totally in control of your life and others? Discuss situations/ circumstances in which you felt you lost control. What was the final outcome?

How important is it for you to be in totally in control of your life and others? Discuss situations/ circumstances in which you felt you lost control. What was the final outcome?

_____
_____
_____
_____
_____
_____
_____
_____
_____
_____
_____
_____
_____
_____
_____
_____
_____
_____
_____
_____
_____
_____
_____
_____
_____
_____
_____
_____
_____
_____
_____
_____
_____
_____
_____
_____
_____
_____
_____

How important is it for you to be in totally in control of your life and others? Discuss situations/ circumstances in which you felt you lost control. What was the final outcome?

How important is it for you to be in totally in control of your life and others? Discuss situations/ circumstances in which you felt you lost control. What was the final outcome?

_____
_____
_____
_____
_____
_____
_____
_____
_____
_____
_____
_____
_____
_____
_____
_____
_____
_____
_____
_____
_____
_____
_____
_____
_____
_____
_____
_____
_____
_____
_____
_____
_____
_____
_____
_____

How important is it for you to be in totally in control of your life and others? Discuss situations/ circumstances in which you felt you lost control. What was the final outcome?

_____
_____
_____
_____
_____
_____
_____
_____
_____
_____
_____
_____
_____
_____
_____
_____
_____
_____
_____
_____
_____
_____
_____
_____
_____
_____
_____
_____
_____
_____
_____
_____
_____
_____
_____
_____

How important is it for you to be in totally in control of your life and others? Discuss situations/ circumstances in which you felt you lost control. What was the final outcome?

_____
_____
_____
_____
_____
_____
_____
_____
_____
_____
_____
_____
_____
_____
_____
_____
_____
_____
_____
_____
_____
_____
_____
_____
_____
_____
_____
_____
_____
_____
_____
_____
_____
_____
_____

Think and write about important/difficult decisions you must take and lay out a plan for approaching each one.

Think and write about important/difficult decisions you must take
and lay out a plan for approaching each one.

Think and write about important/difficult decisions you must take
and lay out a plan for approaching each one.

Think and write about important/difficult decisions you must take and lay out a plan for approaching each one.

_____
_____
_____
_____
_____
_____
_____
_____
_____
_____
_____
_____
_____
_____
_____
_____
_____
_____
_____
_____
_____
_____
_____
_____
_____
_____
_____
_____
_____
_____
_____
_____
_____
_____
_____
_____

What are some of the culture concepts, (your environment) that you feel shapes your life and affects your perception of challenges and the way you overcome them?

What are some of the culture concepts, (your environment) that you feel shapes your life and affects your perception of challenges and the way you overcome them?

_____
_____
_____
_____
_____
_____
_____
_____
_____
_____
_____
_____
_____
_____
_____
_____
_____
_____
_____
_____
_____
_____
_____
_____
_____
_____
_____
_____
_____
_____
_____
_____
_____
_____
_____
_____
_____

What are some of the culture concepts, (your environment) that you feel shapes your life and affects your perception of challenges and the way you overcome them?

_____
_____
_____
_____
_____
_____
_____
_____
_____
_____
_____
_____
_____
_____
_____
_____
_____
_____
_____
_____
_____
_____
_____
_____
_____
_____
_____
_____
_____
_____
_____
_____
_____
_____
_____

What are some of the culture concepts, (your environment) that you feel shapes your life and affects your perception of challenges and the way you overcome them?

_____
_____
_____
_____
_____
_____
_____
_____
_____
_____
_____
_____
_____
_____
_____
_____
_____
_____
_____
_____
_____
_____
_____
_____
_____
_____
_____
_____
_____
_____
_____
_____
_____
_____
_____
_____
_____
_____
_____
_____

What are some of the culture concepts, (your environment) that you feel shapes your life and affects your perception of challenges and the way you overcome them?

What are some of the culture concepts, (your environment) that you feel shapes your life and affects your perception of challenges and the way you overcome them?

What are the spiritual concepts that you feel shapes your life and affects your perception of managing hardships or problems?

_____
_____
_____
_____
_____
_____
_____
_____
_____
_____
_____
_____
_____
_____
_____
_____
_____
_____
_____
_____
_____
_____
_____
_____
_____
_____
_____
_____
_____
_____
_____
_____
_____
_____

What are the spiritual concepts that you feel shapes your life and affects your perception of managing hardships or problems?

_____
_____
_____
_____
_____
_____
_____
_____
_____
_____
_____
_____
_____
_____
_____
_____
_____
_____
_____
_____
_____
_____
_____
_____
_____
_____
_____
_____
_____
_____
_____
_____
_____
_____

What are the spiritual concepts that you feel shapes your life and affects your perception of managing hardships or problems?

_____
_____
_____
_____
_____
_____
_____
_____
_____
_____
_____
_____
_____
_____
_____
_____
_____
_____
_____
_____
_____
_____
_____
_____
_____
_____
_____
_____
_____
_____
_____
_____

What are the spiritual concepts that you feel shapes your life and affects your perception of managing hardships or problems?

_____
_____
_____
_____
_____
_____
_____
_____
_____
_____
_____
_____
_____
_____
_____
_____
_____
_____
_____
_____
_____
_____
_____
_____
_____
_____
_____
_____
_____
_____
_____
_____
_____
_____
_____
_____
_____

What are some of the influences (in the secular world) that seek to control your reactions when it seems your back is against the wall?

_____

_____

_____

_____

_____

_____

_____

_____

_____

_____

_____

_____

_____

_____

_____

_____

_____

_____

_____

_____

_____

_____

_____

_____

_____

_____

_____

_____

_____

_____

What are some of the influences (in the secular world) that seek to control your reactions when it seems your back is against the wall?

_____

_____

_____

_____

_____

_____

_____

_____

_____

_____

_____

_____

_____

_____

_____

_____

_____

_____

_____

_____

_____

_____

_____

_____

_____

_____

_____

_____

_____

_____

_____

_____

_____

_____

_____

_____

What are some of the influences (in the secular world) that seek to control your reactions when it seems your back is against the wall?

What are some of the influences (in the secular world) that seek to control your reactions when it seems your back is against the wall?

_____
_____
_____
_____
_____
_____
_____
_____
_____
_____
_____
_____
_____
_____
_____
_____
_____
_____
_____
_____
_____
_____
_____
_____
_____
_____
_____
_____
_____
_____
_____
_____
_____
_____
_____
_____
_____

Outline some of the reasons you do not trust yourself. Talk about the last promise you made to yourself, if you kept the promise or not, and how you felt afterwards.

_____
_____
_____
_____
_____
_____
_____
_____
_____
_____
_____
_____
_____
_____
_____
_____
_____
_____
_____
_____
_____
_____
_____
_____
_____
_____
_____
_____
_____
_____
_____
_____
_____
_____
_____
_____
_____
_____

Outline some of the reasons you do not trust yourself. Talk about the last promise you made to yourself, if you kept the promise or not, and how you felt afterwards.

_____
_____
_____
_____
_____
_____
_____
_____
_____
_____
_____
_____
_____
_____
_____
_____
_____
_____
_____
_____
_____
_____
_____
_____
_____
_____
_____
_____
_____
_____
_____
_____
_____
_____
_____

Outline some of the reasons you do not trust yourself. Talk about the last promise you made to yourself, if you kept the promise or not, and how you felt afterwards.

Outline some of the reasons you do not trust yourself. Talk about the last promise you made to yourself, if you kept the promise or not, and how you felt afterwards.

How can you change your view and learn to trust yourself?

_____
_____
_____
_____
_____
_____
_____
_____
_____
_____
_____
_____
_____
_____
_____
_____
_____
_____
_____
_____
_____
_____
_____
_____
_____
_____
_____
_____
_____
_____
_____
_____

How can you change your view and learn to trust yourself?

_____
_____
_____
_____
_____
_____
_____
_____
_____
_____
_____
_____
_____
_____
_____
_____
_____
_____
_____
_____
_____
_____
_____
_____
_____
_____
_____
_____
_____
_____
_____
_____

ⁱ Warren, Rick. <u>The Purpose Driven Life</u>. Zondervan: (Grand Rapids, 2002) pg.107.

ⁱⁱ Chew, Robert. "How I Got Screwed by Bernie Madoff". <u>Time Magazine</u> 15 December 2008. January

18 2009.
<http://www.time.com/time/business/article/0,8599,1866398,00.html?xid=newsletter-weekly>.

ⁱⁱⁱ Chew, Robert. "How I Got Screwed by Bernie Madoff". <u>Time Magazine</u> 15 December 2008. January

18 2009.
<http://www.time.com/time/business/article/0,8599,1866398,00.html?xid=newsletter-weekly>.

^{iv} Nelson, Thomas. <u>Holy, Bible King James Version.</u> Nashville Tennessee: Thomas Nelson Publishers,

2006. pg.737.

^v Alirlandee , Abunoor. <u>Imam Wallace Warith Deen Mohammed (1933-2008).</u> Abu Noor

Al-Irlandee Unrepentant Fenian Islamist 09 October 2008.15 February 2009.

http://abunooralirlandee.wordpress.com/2008/09/10/imam-wallace-warith-deen-mohammed-1933-2008/.

^{vi} Author, Unknown. "Farewells: Malcolm X." <u>Unique Cars and Parts</u> .Web.15 Apr 2009.

<http://www.uniquecarsandparts.com.au/farewells_malcolm_x.htm>.

^{vii} Nelson, Thomas. <u>Holy, Bible King James Version</u>. Nashville Tennessee: (Thomas

Nelson Publishers, 2006.) pg.743.

^{viii} Nelson, Thomas. <u>Holy, Bible King James Version</u>. Nashville Tennessee: (Thomas

Nelson Publishers, 2006.) pg.1116.

^{ix} Sapp, Priscilla. <u>Pillar of Prayer in Eastern Africa.</u> Global Strategy. (23 March 2009.)

<http://www.imb.org/strategist/Prayer/pillar_of_prayer_e_africa_print_version.htm>.

^x Garmin. <u>What is GPS</u>. 2009. Garmin Ltd. (16 February 2009).<http.//www.8.garmin.com/aboutGPS/>.

^{xi} Reader's Version, New International. <u>Holy Bible New International Reader's Version.</u> Colorado Springs:

(International Bible Society, 1996). pg.4.

^{xii} Reader's Version, New International. <u>Holy Bible New International Reader's Version.</u> Colorado Springs:

(International Bible Society, 1996). pg.4 – 5.

[xiii] Pickett, Joseph P. et al.. <u>The American Heritage® Dictionary of the English Language.</u> <u>4th</u> ed. Boston:

  Boston: Houghton Mifflin Company, 2000.

[xiv] Wikipedia, the free encyclopedia, <u>Spirituality</u>. 2009. Wikipedia. Web.15 Apr 2009.

  <http://en.wikipedia.org/wiki/Spirituality>.

[xv] Armstrong , Karen. <u>A History of God</u>. Vintage London: Random House, 1999. pg. 49.

[xvi] Wikipedia, the free encyclopedia, <u>Polemic.</u> 2009. Wikipedia. Web.15 March 2009.

  < http://en.wikipedia.org/wiki/Polemic>.

[xvii] Armstrong , Karen. <u>A History of God</u>. Vintage London: Random House, 1999. pg 65.

[xviii] Thiessen, C. Henry. <u>Lectures in Systematic Theology</u>. Rev. ed. Eerdmans: Grand Rapids: 1979. pg.32

[xix] Thiessen, C. Henry. <u>Lectures in Systematic Theology</u>. Rev. ed. Eerdmans: Grand Rapids: 1979. pg.33

[xx] Thiessen, C. Henry. <u>Lectures in Systematic Theology</u>. Rev. ed. Eerdmans: Grand Rapids: 1979. pg.34

[xxi] Thiessen, C. Henry. <u>Lectures in Systematic Theology</u>. Rev. ed. Eerdmans: Grand Rapids: 1979. pg.35

[xxii] Thiessen, C. Henry. <u>Lectures in Systematic Theology</u>. Rev. ed. Eerdmans: Grand Rapids: 1979. pg.37

[xxiii] Wikipedia, the free encyclopedia, <u>Polemic.</u> 2009. Wikipedia. Web.15 March 2009.

  <<u>http://en.wikipedia.org/wiki/Polytheistic</u>>.

[21] Albright, Wlliam Fox.<u> From The Stone Age To Christianity Monotheism And The Historical Process</u>.

  Baltimore: The John Hopkins Press, 1940.

[22] Metzger, Bruce. M. <u>The Oxford Companion to the</u> Bible . Oxford: (Oxford University Press, 1997).

  pg. 513, 649.

[23] Esposito, John L. <u>What Everyone Needs to Know about Islam</u>. Oxford: (Oxford University Press, 2002).

  pg.17

[24] Esposito, John L. <u>What Everyone Needs to Know about Islam</u>. Oxford: (Oxford University Press, 2002).

  pg.111,112,118

[xxiv] Cary, Jolinda. "What is Spirituality?." 29,April 2009 Web.20 May 2009.

  <http://alternativespirituality.suite101.com/article.cfm/whatisspirituality>.

xxix Wikipedia, the free encyclopedia, Judaism. 2009. Wikipedia. Web.15 March 2009.

<http://en.wikipedia.org/wiki/Judaism>.

xxx Berry, Mary Thomas. "Buddhism."Twenthieth Century Encyclopedia of Catholocism. 1st ed. 1967.

xxxi Wikipedia, the free encyclopedia, Buddhism. 2009. Wikipedia. Web.15 March 2009.

<http://en.wikipedia.org/wiki/Buddhism>.

xxxii J. Zavos, "Defending Hindu Traditio": Sanatana Dharma as a Symbol of Orthodoxy in Colonial India,

Religion .Volume 31, Number 2, April 2001, pp. 109-123

xxxiiiAdherents, "Major Religions of the World." Adherents.com Web.16 Apr 2009.

<http://www.adherents.com/Religions_By_Adherents.html>.

xxxiv Osborne, E, Accessing R.E. Founders & Leaders, Buddhism, Hinduism and Sikhism Teacher's Book

Mainstream.. (Folens Limited, 2005) pg.9

xxxv Buswell, Robert E. "Buddhism". Encyclopedia of Buddhism. New York.2003. pg. 383

xxxviPaul, Margaret. "Trust Starts With You". Inner Bonding . 31 December 2006.

<http://www.innerbonding.com/show-article/649/trust-starts-with-you.html>

xxxvii Reader's Version, New International. Holy Bible New International Reader's Version. Colorado Springs:

(International Bible Society, 1996). pg.895.

xxxviii Gene Mims, The kingdom focused church (Tennessee, Nashville 2003) pg 6.

xxxix ED Wheat, Love life for every married couple (Michigan, Grand Rapids 1980) 203.

xl Gene Mims, The kingdom focused church (Tennessee, Nashville 2003) 135.

xli Gene Mims, The kingdom focused church (Tennessee, Nashville 2003) 137

xlii Frizzell, Gregory. Returning to Holiness. Fulton: The Master Design, 2000.pg.67

xliii Reader's Version, New International. Holy Bible New International Reader's Version. Colorado Springs:

(International Bible Society, 1996). pg.456.

xliv Reader's Version, New International. Holy Bible New International Reader's Version. Colorado Springs:

(International Bible Society, 1996). pg.1539.

xlv Reader's Version, New International. Holy Bible New International Reader's Version. Colorado Springs:

(International Bible Society, 1996). pg.1554.

[xlvi] Reader's Version, New International. <u>Holy Bible New International Reader's Version.</u> Colorado Springs:

(International Bible Society, 1996). pg.1647.

[xlvii] Reader's Version, New International. <u>Holy Bible New International Reader's Version.</u> Colorado Springs:

(International Bible Society, 1996). pg.1507.

[xlviii] Whitney Donald S.. Simplify Your Spiritual Life (Colorado Springs, Colo.: NavPress, 2003).

http://biblicalspirituality.org/takeup.html.

[xlix] Guralink, David. "Distraction."Webster's Dictionary. 1985. (409)

[l] Brand,Draper,England, Chad,Charles,Archie. Holman Bible Dictionary. <u>Concupiscence.</u> Nashville,

Tennessee. 2004.pg. 326

[li] Nettles, Robert. "Spiritual Distractions." (Virtual Christian Magazine 2007).

http://vcmagazine.org/article.aspx?volume=9&issue=1&article=distractions

[lii] Nettles, Robert. "Spiritual Distractions." (Virtual Christian Magazine 2007).

http://vcmagazine.org/article.aspx?volume=9&issue=1&article=distractions

[liii] Nettles, Robert. "Spiritual Distractions." (Virtual Christian Magazine 2007).

http://vcmagazine.org/article.aspx?volume=9&issue=1&article=distractions

[liv] Guralink, David. <u>Desire</u> Webster's Dictionary. 1985. (1208)

[lv] Hendryx, <u>John. Is it God's Desire for All Men to Be Saved?</u> . Monergism.

http://www.monergism.com/thethreshold/articles/onsite/desireallsaved.html

DO IT GODS WAY!

Made in the USA
Lexington, KY
03 September 2017